"The Prince or the Predator is an easy, insightful read that helps readers understand the actions of the predator in relationships, yet provides readers with useful strategies and affirmations to transform ourselves and create the relationships we desire. I recommend this book to everyone who wants to have successful relationships."

—Ann Davis, Ph.D.
Alliant International University

"This book is a must to read by those coping with difficult relationships and those in the helping profession."

—Kenneth Harper, Ph.D.

"This book offers a good practical guide in addressing a serious topic."

—Steve R. Brown, Esq.

-Damation-

The Art of Successful Relationships

The Prince
or
the Predator

Georgina Ramirez, M.A.

VANTAGE PRESS
New York

FIRST EDITION

Copyright © 2010 by Georgina Ramirez, M.A.

Published by Vantage Press, Inc.
419 Park Ave. South, New York, NY 10016

Manufactured in the United States of America
ISBN: 978-0-533-16171-3

Library of Congress Catalog Card No: 2008911413

0 9 8 7 6 5 4 3 2 1

Dedication

To my children, Christopher and Gina Stephanie.

> *You are the greatest gift of all,*
> *Your loving presence in my life inspired*
> *and unfolded the great dimensions in my life.*

In memorium to my mother, Maria Hanaco

> *A woman of graceful courage, integrity, and*
> *undoubted faith.*
> *A true inspirational role model for which I was*
> *blessed.*

Contents

Acknowledgments   ix
Introduction   xi
A Note to Readers   xv

I: Understanding Human Nature
The Biology of Nature   3
The Predator—The Oppressor   8
The Victim   14
The Frog and the Scorpion   24

II: The Battlefield or the Playground?
Know Where You Stand   29
The Game of Life   31
Identifying the Traps   34
Identifying the Traps   38
Know Your Opponent   41
Know Your Weakness   47
Place Yourself in a Position of Power   50
Never Underestimate Your Opponent   57

III: Awakening Your Inner Strength
Beyond Social Conditioning   61
Sense of Purpose   64
Make a Plan that Works for You   68
Focus—Keep Your Eye on the Ball   72
Support and Self-Nurturing   74

IV: Manifesting Your True Power
Love—The Power of Transformation   81

Resources   93

Acknowledgments

Thank you to Ruth, Kenneth, Darby and Dennis for their support and encouragement in the writing of this book.

My infinite appreciation to Reverend Mark Trotter for his kindness, patience, and intelligent debates. It made this a much better book.

My forever gratitude to the ones that have paved the way before me throughout the beginning of times.

Introduction

Why do we get hurt and betrayed by the ones we trust and love the most? Why are we still exhibiting such harmful behavior after thousands of years of praying, meditating, building churches, and achieving scientific and technological advances in our civilized culture?

Like many others, I am still puzzled by these questions. However, looking for scientific answers to explain the origin of this behavior is not the intent of this book. There are too many gaps in our knowledge and the history of mankind to absolutely determine the roots of this destructive behavior. Since the history of our past is still in fragments, and the secrets of our brain are still yet to be found, this writer will not attempt to discuss or establish it's origin, but to strengthen individuals to cope and succeed in difficult relationships.

In this book, I use the term *"predator"* as a metaphor to represent abusive behavior. A *predator* is an individual who seduces and later abuses the well-being of his victim. He seeks to pleasure himself as he totally disregards the needs and desires of his prey. He leaves his victim confused and exhausted, while he himself grows stronger and satisfied. It is the desire of this oppressor to achieve full and absolute control over his prey as his survival depends on the complete submission and emotional destruction of his victim. His dominant power and control is often justified as appropriate and necessary.

This emotional and psychological abuse is usually denied, overlooked, and frequently perceived as not important, yet it is extremely damaging to the human mind. It is my aim to increase awareness of the dangers and specific ways of this manipulative behavior, and to offer effective and practical tools to help those who might be, or have been, victimized by this *oppressor* whether in their personal relationships, business, or professional lives. I wish to help them identify and recognize his seductive ways, as well as to give them the tools to learn how to successfully deal and cope with this oppressor. In addition, and equally important, is to help identify the common traits of victims—the beliefs and characteristics that makes them become an easy prey for this *oppressor,* and how to change and empower them in overcoming these traits.

In business and in my professional experience as a psychotherapist, I have found that the power of the *oppressor* is often mystifying and misunderstood by the victim and the *oppressor* himself. You will find that this *oppressor* has a false identity and a root core belief that, once understood by the victim, it will unlock a powerful force within the prey. This will not only open the gate to gracefully defeat this opponent, but also gives the power to lead the way.

Finally, in chapters three and four I present the solution to being seduced and manipulated by having and practicing a strong spiritual and moral core. When one develops such a strong center, one is not swayed by the constant seduction of the *oppressor,* whether manifested by an individual, group, or culture and thus not being put into the position of being victimized by those who would take advantage of us. Furthermore, by tapping into this new awareness, the reader will be placed in a position of true power where the possibilities of absolute fulfillment in life are endless and only limited by his or her own decisions.

May this book bring more light and understanding by helping individuals succeed in their true and transcendental work by becoming the true force behind the fine and divine wheel of creation.

A Note to Readers

The content of this book is my personal opinion based on my observations, readings, and experience. It does not constitute professional advice. My advice would be if needed, to seek professional counseling.

It is my intention and expectations that the information and strategies included will be used appropriately and with the purpose for which they were intended.

The names used in the examples cited throughout the book are fictitious.

Finally, please note that although I have used the words "he," "him," and other "gender-specific" references, this is NOT to imply that abuse is, in any way, gender specific, but only to aid the reader rather than going back and forth between "he" and "she," "him" and "her." Abuse is related to *both* genders and should be kept in mind while reading this book.

The Art of Successful
Relationships

I
Understanding Human Nature

The Biology of Nature

Nature's Basic Instincts

The *predator* is an ancient symbol, an *oppressor* and destroyer of the human mind. His dominant nature may be manifested in an individual, a specific group, or a culture. These negative characteristics may also be represented by the values and beliefs of a particular society, geared to mislead and keep humans trapped in fear, preventing them from overcoming and transcending the primitive human nature's response to react and perform in order to assure survival. In an individual, this energy is usually identified by an inflated ego and a castrating and arbitrary need to have complete control and power over others at any cost.

This need for absolute power and control over others may appear in both male and female, but due to the dominant nature of this behavior, is it more easily associated with males. As man has been given a natural drive to hunt, he may be more prompted to manifest this aggressive and dominant behavior. Consider that since ancient times, hunting for food has been a survival mechanism that has contributed to the continuation of the human race; and man's success in hunting produced a sense of power and control over the animal kingdom.

Furthermore, hunting and pride in the courageous conquest of his prey have not only secured man's survival but gave him the courage to succeed in life. This courage and success in hunting protected and empowered the human race as individuals worked together, but this courage becomes a deceptive trait that destroys life when it is used only to indulge in self-gratification. This is a trait of the *oppressor* of life.

As humans evolved, ways of coping with life's problems have become more civilized as we developed intelligent methods and more effective skills to survive and succeed in life, including cooperation versus repression. Consequently, a more sophisticated and efficient neurological connection has been established in our brain, giving us the potential to use reasoning at levels far above primary instincts. This is known as decision-making. Nonetheless, since the instinctual drive to survive is deeply rooted in the limbic system which is the most primitive and emotional part of the brain; when threatened, we experience fear. This fear will activate this automatic and emotional drive which can often overrule our reasoning.* Thus, leaving us at the mercy of our emotions and defensively reacting to life.

Once a hunter, how an individual reacts to the events in life will depend directly on his level of maturity and his level of reasoning. The ability to reason differentiates humans from animals. Our potential for reasoning, for discerning the truth, for thinking about the consequences of our behavior places us on a higher plane. It is quite interesting to note that most *oppressors* are often unaware of their own abusive behavior. Furthermore, they usually have no awareness of how their behavior affects others.

*Daniel Goleman, Ph.D. (1995). Emotional Intelligence. New York, U.S.A.

In my practice as a psychotherapist, I have found that the *oppressor's* lack of self-awareness is one of the most difficult barriers to overcome. This *oppressor* often perceives his abusive behavior as appropriate and righteous. He believes the harm he does to others is in "self defense." He arbitrarily blames others for his behavior.

Primitive instincts are an innate part of basic human nature and they are emotionally based. They are unconscious, instinctive and impulsive. They certainly played an important role in securing our survival in ancient times, and they are deeply embedded in us. Our instincts are based on our need to avoid pain and gain pleasure. These emotions have ruled our lives and will continue to do so, unless we use our intelligence. We can do this by reasoning and taking time to think about what is truly in our best interest and not by what looks, sounds or feels good.

It becomes a problem when we insist on maintaining and continuing to use the same automatic and instinctive emotional drive to respond to the complexities of our world. In contemporary times, we no longer react to the elements of nature as we once did; instead, we often react to sophisticated and at times deceitful information spread throughout our society. As man no longer needs to hunt for food to survive, now he is hunting for the power that money provides; the power to secure his survival in these times. Money and the power have become the means to an end for achieving control and assuring self-survival. In the modern world, it is easy to be confused and misled by faulty information we see, hear, and read; that information is not always the truth, but it is presented to us in ways geared to make us think, want and act as others desire. This spread of misinformation can trigger the emotion of fear inside us, the fear that we may not have enough power or money to fulfill our desires. Often we are confused, burdened with artificial needs such as a bigger house, a new Mercedes, and more goodies on our shelves, as we are conditioned to believe that material possessions secure our happiness. In our frenzied need to chase this carrot, we often fail to fulfill our authentic needs such as to love, to be loved, and accepted for who we truly are.

On the other hand, as the demands and circumstances in our society have changed, the methods we use to cope and respond need to change in order to adapt and succeed. We can acknowledge and understand that our minds can be easily triggered by fear to function at a very primitive level. We are bound to react.

In order to succeed, we must define and set our own priorities straight and be determined to stand by them.

For example, an individual like the *oppressor* who fearfully reacts to life instead of thinking, his responses will be often unpredictable and inconsistent. Reacting defensively to life will keep this volatile individual angry and resentful; living a life in which he is never satisfied, blaming others and ashamed of himself. These emotion will keep him trapped in an endless circle of running hard and hiding from the sun, escaping from his own freedom.

This book is not about a perfect world and the wishful thinking of make-believe. This book is for you to regain control of your life by knowing who you really are. It is for you to rediscover your own wisdom and strength to create and obtain what you want out of life. Once you understand the nature of this *oppressor,* you will be able to identify and use the strategies that most fit your circumstances and turn things around to your benefit. You will see results.

Throughout this book, I mostly refer to the *oppressor*

as "he." I acknowledge the fact that although this abusive and oppressive behavior is **not particular** to any gender, it is more prevalent in males and it is exhibited more often by males as we can see it by the number of males in prison and male perpetrators of domestic violence: "90 to ninety-five percent of domestic violence victims are women."** "As many as ninety-five percent of domestic violence perpetrators are male"*** "The chance of being victimized by an intimate is ten times greater for a woman than a man."****

An *oppressor*—man or woman—can function at different levels of harm. Emotional injuries can have a deep and harmful lasting effect in our lives which can lead us into self-destruction. If this is the case, strongly recommend seeking professional help.

**Bureau of Justice: Violence Between Intimates (NCJ–149259) 1994.
***Institute of Justice and U.S. Department of Health and Human Services 1995.
****Bureau of Justice: National Crime Victimization Survey 1994.

The Predator—The Oppressor

Freedom and reason make us man—take this away and what are we then?
—Shakespeare

In the context of this book, a *predator* is an individual, man or woman, who abuses his victim for his own pleasure and satisfaction, and disregards the victim's needs and desires. He leaves his victim confused, feeling hopeless and powerless while he himself grows stronger and more self-satisfied.

This kind of individual can be all around; they hide themselves behind the mask of a civilized, successful, loving, and caring individual. Knowing how to talk, how to look, and how to deceive, they are always on the hunt, chasing their prey. Once he traps and deceives his prey, he abuses her without regret. This behavior is just the manifestation of the *oppressor's* basic instinct which is temporarily satisfied until he preys on his next victim.

The *oppressor's* behavior is simple—chase the prey, use it, and destroy it. It does not matter if the prey is a person or an object, what matters to this *oppressor* is the pleasure of having total power and control over his victim, which gives him a sense of importance and security.

Because his need for survival and his sense of identity are based on the degree of control that he has over others, the fear of losing control is easily triggered when things don't go his way. This fear-based perception is deeply rooted in his mind and is seated in an unconscious automatic drive that can be triggered by anyone who appears to move, think, and feel different. Once the *oppressor* feels vulnerable and unsafe he will resort to drastic measures to protect himself, from using simple tactics of intimidation such as angry gestures, to verbal threats, and sometimes escalating into physical violence. And, unless he consciously decides to reason and behave different, he will revert back to his basic primitive mode when he feels threatened, viciously and cruelly attacking his victim whether his perception is real or not.

It is not that the instinctive drive to hunt in order to survive has become unhealthy, nor it is the pursuit of material success that enhances his life; what is unhealthy is the *oppressor's* perceptions and actions to fulfill his self-centered desires by totally subordinating others to him. Our society appears to have done a good job at keeping mankind hunting with an absolute need for total control. He is conditioned to believe that the more material possessions he accumulates, the greater his physical performance, and the more power he has over others, the more secure his survival is in our society. This often triggers the fear to not succeed and we accelerate to have the biggest house, the new Mercedes, and more goodies on our shelves to feel safe. These beliefs can keep a man hunting without control and exiled from his true happiness and purpose in life. The more he stands on these beliefs, the more fragile his identity will be, the more fearful he can become as his sense of identity depends on material success.

This reactive way of living life under fear deprives man of his true source of happiness, thus preventing him

from achieving a satisfied and fulfilled life, a life of substance, a life he designs and lives from within. Instead, he
spends his life obsessed with achieving external power
and control. Deceived by his fellow man and powerful corporations who appeal to his senses and promise him excitement and happiness, he blindly falls into their web of
deception and indulges his senses even more. He gives in
to the sweet temptation of external success and achieves
a false sense of security by building his identity on material possessions and outside power while submitting others to his domain. However, following this self-indulgent
path means that there is a price to pay, and the *oppressor*
cannot and will not escape the consequences of violating
the natural laws and universal principles that rule life
and his true nature without harming himself. The more
power and control he achieves over his victim, the further
he will fall into the shadows of his own sick ignorance and
self-centeredness. In time, probably sooner rather than
later, he will realize that what he has done to others will
be done to him. It is just a matter of time.

The fact is that as this *oppressor* asserts his dominant power over others, deep down inside he feel unsafe.
He perceives the world as hostile and unpredictable. He
compensates for his feelings of insecurity and shame by
portraying a false image of a strong individual who is superior to everyone else, and who is always in control. At
the same time, he deeply doubts his ability to become that
ideal man. This conflictive and egocentric image of himself causes a deep sense of fear and an absolute need to
control not only his surroundings but the people in his
life. This includes you. This dominant control is often rationalized and justified by the *oppressor* as being in your
"best interest." He believes that he knows better than
anyone else and he is always "right."

As his need for control increases, he is terrified when he feel criticized or rejected. He experiences continuous fear of the unknown in a dangerous world. This distorted perception reinforces the *oppressor's* need for absolute power and control, thus ensuring his perceived illusion of being separated and superior to all while guaranteeing his self-created unhappiness.

The Predator's Traits

The following are some of the common traits and natural characteristics of this *oppressor:*

- Self-centered
- Insecure
- Incapable of self-awareness
- Highly competitive
- Incapable of being sensitive to the needs of others
- Emotionally unavailable
- Unable to take responsibility
- An irrational, arbitrary, and circular thinker

The methods this individual uses to obtain complete power and control over others vary from apparent sweet coercion to direct verbal and physical intimidation. The core of his identity is based on shame and fear, and he constantly needs to reassure himself and others that he is better and knows more than anyone else. He is highly competitive in his attempts to relate to others, and he appears aloof and disconnected as he asserts his delusions of grandeur and omnipotence. He is always right, because he arbitrarily declares so and orders so. Whatever he dogmatically asserts must be, and it exists regardless of any evidence to the contrary because—and only because—he thinks so. He is self-absorbed, he exists in his own world, and he blames others for his own actions and feelings. He cannot be accountable for his own behavior; he is easily angered and enraged.

Whatever he decides is an absolute and final conclusion. He perceives any different opinion as defiant, irrational, and threatening to his existence, regardless of whether this opinion has merit. Whatever he thinks and says actually exists, and that is all that exists. Any different opinion is automatically perceived as coming from the "enemy," and this "enemy" must be destroyed, sooner rather than later.

John: A profile of predatory behavior

A man in his early forties, the manager of a successful company, John was married to Betty. They lived in a middle-upper-class home with their two children, four and seven years old. John loved and took pride in having achieved the American dream: owning a beautiful home and driving a brand-new Mercedes. John believed in the traditional role of woman, which he interpreted as exercising complete control over his wife. He maintained total control over their finances and family decisions. All expenses, including groceries, were to be approved and reimbursed with proof of purchase.

John believed in saving for retirement, but he could not control his addiction to alcohol and his daily compulsion to buy and collect expensive baseball cards.

He justified the accumulation of baseball cards as an investment for the future, which he charged to his credit cards, building up debt. John did not support his wife's in-

terest in education, but demanded that she work and give him her paycheck, claiming he knew more about financial management. John's wife, Betty, was expected to take care of the house and children, make a living and never disagree. John believed that his children should show respect by being obedient to him and maintaining silence. He believed that an arbitrary and authoritarian model of parenting was destined to make him a successful father.

John feared getting fat, and in his need to control his environment, he prohibited doughnuts, cookies, and any other "junk" food from entering their house. He watched over the eating patterns of his wife and children and constantly reminded them how fat they could get, although none of them were fat. John worked hard to keep everything under control, which often gave him an excuse to reprimand his wife and children. John responded with threats of divorce to Betty's attempts to influence his beliefs and behavior. Betty reacted fearfully by ending the conversation and appeasing John with his favorite vodka drink. John maintained control.

John also feared losing his high-paying job along with the status and lifestyle that he had worked so hard for over twenty years to achieve. He had trouble sleeping, and he spent the rest of the time in front of his computer. Aloof and disconnected from the world around him, John could not understand why people failed to appreciate him when he advised them in how to live their lives. After all, he knew what was best and he had succeeded in corporate world . . .

The Victim

The more we deny and relinquish our own needs to please others, the more vulnerable we become.

Once upon a time . . . whether you were sixteen, twenty or forty, you awakened one day to realize that you were no longer in heaven. How did this happen? You were so happy, dancing in the full ecstasy of life, but suddenly you felt afraid, angry, resentful, and perhaps even fearful of your own future. How did the one you trusted the most become an enemy in your life?

He spoke sweet-sounding words and you believed them. He seduced your innocence and you are now placed in his domain. Your trust has been betrayed. He has charmed you by enchanting your senses and accommodating your desires.

Now there is only fear, pain, and intimidation by the

14

oppressor. Whether it is at home, work or in business, your trust has been betrayed. How did this happen? How did you get caught in this trap? Where did those sweet promises go?

How many fairy tales and stories have we heard where innocence has been destroyed? How many tears have we seen? How much pain and suffering should one endure before we wake up to reclaim our own birthright to be treated with love and respect, and not with threats and intimidation?

But what makes a woman an easy prey for the *oppressor*? As a woman has learned and developed her role to take care of the needs of others, she tends to overlook her own needs. Most messages for women have been a list of "should" and "should not" on how to be a "good woman" and a "good caregiver." Young girls are taught to be "good, trusting, and nice to others." After all, isn't this a "safe" world? And what should a good wife and mother be? She is taught to be sensitive, loving, responsible, faithful, and agreeable. Many of these are good qualities, however, some of these beliefs can easily mislead women. No doubt these messages have good intentions, but it has been said that the road to hell is often paved with good intentions.

Women are expected to get married, have children, and live happily ever after. As the fairy tale goes, she deeply desires in her heart to be loved. She believes her needs and desires will be taken care of by a strong, loving, and handsome prince who one day will come. All that a woman needs to do is to find the right prince.

With this perception and assumed beliefs, a woman can become an easy prey for the *oppressor* who is looking for the vulnerable and potential victim. Nonetheless, she thinks, if he looks like a prince, moves like a prince, talks like a prince . . . he should be a prince! Shouldn't he?

Women's desire to belong, to be loved, and to be appreciated can induce women to become an easy target for an *oppressor.* The more needy and insecure a woman is, the more enticing and vulnerable she becomes for this *oppressor.* He will make her fully dependent on him and she will be easily manipulated and controlled by fear—the fear of abandonment, fear of rejection, and fear of no financial support. This is how this dominant individual comes alive. He keeps her in fear and nurtures himself by draining the vital energy of life from his victim.

He will first seduce her innocence by becoming and portraying all of what she ever dreamed and by meeting her "desires" and "expectations." He will pursue her to satisfy himself, to be affirmed, and to feel validated; not to offer his love and strength. And what does she get? She gets . . . exhausted! Her world spins around him as he is to be, and ought to be, her universe. She is to spin out of control at the snap of his fingers, for he believes he is to be the one, the Master of All.

For the one who is dealing with this *oppressor,* the hesitance to express her feelings for fear of retribution is well known and painfully experienced every day; the deep silence and the mask that covers her pain, the feeling of shame, is only known to her. Every day she "walks on eggshells" in fear of trigging his anger; slowly dying in her soul she keeps falling deeper and deeper into the *oppressor's* controlling web, the *predator* of her mind, the *oppressor* of her soul.

Sofia: A profile of a victim

I met Sofia at one of my groups. Sofia was an attractive and beautiful woman in her early thirties. She was looking down and remained extremely quiet for most of the time we were in our group session. After much encouragement, she shared her story, which I will never forget; and it still gives me chills.

Sofia had been married to a police officer for over five years, she had no children, and her husband did not allow her to work. She had been the victim of emotional, physical, and sexual abuse by her husband who knew how to inflict internal physical injuries which left no visible marks on Sofia's body. As a result, she could not prove the physical abuse to the authorities. He had assured her that the police would not believe her since he worked for law enforcement and knew how to deceive the system. Sofia feared for her life. For years she suffered this abuse in silence and feared that her life would abruptly end. The day I met Sofia, she had contacted a higher authority in law enforcement who immediately placed her under protective services. That afternoon, Sofia was going to be taken to an undisclosed location where a new identity would be created for her to start her life over. I never saw Sofia again, yet the fear in her eyes and the deadly silence of her soul stayed with me.

Physical and sexual abuse is not the scope of this book. In cases of physical and sexual abuse, I strongly recommend contacting the authorities and professionals competent in dealing with these types of cases. However, this book is intended for those who are dealing with emotional abuse, the loss of their vital life energy.

As a woman tries to be a "good woman" by taking care of the needs of others, she often extends herself by trying harder to be "good enough." In her effort to succeed, she often denies her own needs by living a make-believe life pretending to be happy and hoping that her pain will go away. The more she denies and relinquishes her own needs and desires to please others, the more she becomes extremely vulnerable to be abused by others. She subjects herself to be a victim of abusive behavior. The consequence of being caught in the *oppressor's* trap, to be under his dominant power and control, is a painful injury to a woman's basic instincts which is the loss of contact with the force of life within her.

As the victim feels overwhelmed and as her pain increases, her desperate attempt to cover it leads her to fall into depression and into other traps of life, such as having secret relationships, becoming obsessive compulsive or addicted to sex, drugs, alcohol, and food. As the victim seeks the quick fix to numb her senses, her pain is hidden as she slowly, but surely, drifts down into the unconscious stream of life, losing her true nature, her true identity.

Perhaps, you may keep telling yourself, "maybe if I just give a little bit more, everything will be all right; if I just work harder." For a short time, this seems to work. The *oppressor* starts looking like a charming prince again, but then he demands more and more which leaves you exhausted and with nowhere to go. Besides "**it's all your fault**," he says over and over again. In our need to overcome the feelings of shame and guilt we often end up overextending ourselves to prove that we are worth loving, that we are "good enough" . . . and you wonder why you are tired? Perhaps even depressed?

Rose: A profile of a victim

She was an attractive, intelligent and friendly woman in her late thirties, a housewife, and a proud mother of two loving and intelligent children five and seven years old. She had been married for over twelve years to a loving and successful businessman. She came to see me because she could not understand why she was feeling depressed after having everything a woman could ever dream of having. She lived an upper middle class lifestyle and enjoyed her friends and family. I saw nothing wrong with this picture, until I realized that in her effort to support, understand and prove her love to her husband she had slowly been sucked into the trap of believing and accepting her husband's pleadings to have sex with other men he had selected. He then required her to share all the details with him claiming that "it was good for their marriage." His persuasive work, was not completed in one day. It started as a simple joke by asking her to smile and flirt with the man across the table, and over time it evolved into a most bizarre and unhealthy situation in which she was having sex with different men every two or three weeks. She tried to stop, but he kept asking her to help him feel good by doing it one more time. She loved her husband, and she wanted him to be happy, which he was. When she came to see me, her guilt was overwhelming as she didn't have the strength to continue fulfilling his desires, she was exhausted, and felt trapped. Rose feared her marriage would break up along with her emotional well-being. She had thought about committing suicide.

It has always amazed me to observe that the biggest trick that an *oppressor* has ever pulled is to convince the prey that the emotional or physical injuries that are inflicted on the victim are for "*your own good*" as well as for the good of the relationship . . .

Robert: A victim's profile

A successful and intelligent man in his early fifties, Robert lived in an upper middle class home with his young and beautiful wife, Mary Jane. Robert was a faithful, hardworking, and loving man who struggled to keep his two jobs while meeting his wife's expensive lifestyle. During their marriage, Mary Jane had a couple of affairs which she denied. She blamed Robert for his lack of understanding as the reason for her affairs. She compared Robert with their wealthier friends and often criticized him for not performing as a "man." Mary Jane loved to flirt with Robert's friends. She saw nothing wrong with flirting as she perceived it as being "friendly." After all, "it was all Robert's fault." Robert feared losing his beautiful and seductive wife as he blamed himself for the problems in their marriage.

As mentioned before, abusive behavior is not specific to any gender. Living with an *oppressive* man or woman—forces you to live a life that is dominated by fear. Living under fear is a dangerous state of being, as it robs you of your strength and your vital life energy.

*   *   *

The Old Bug: the Impostor of Low Self Worth.

If you were born in an ideal society, you are prone to carry "the old bug" that causes and sustains low self-esteem which is most likely developed in childhood. Low self-esteem or low self-worth is frequently used in our society to indicate lack of confidence. I have often wondered if this could just be part of our normal development as a result of living in a somewhat confused double-bind society, based on "do as I say, not as I do"?

As we were growing up, in our effort to fit in and to be accepted, we learned that we needed to suppress our senses, to give up our identity and to become a false image of who we really are. In attempting to fulfill this image, we begin to feel ashamed of ourselves, as we feel we may not be good enough, thin enough, or rich enough. This process is usually unconscious, but still painful as it is geared to deny our true self.

These beliefs of low self-worth serve as a frame of reference for the rest of our lives. Dealing with an *oppressor* can trigger strong feelings of low self-worth and insecurity which can be devastating in many ways.

Remember that nothing will destroy our emotional security more quickly than loving or dealing with someone who has an extreme, unhealthy, and narcissistic need for reassurance. Alcoholics, compulsive disorders, narcissistic and borderline personalities are the most energy draining and exhausting relationships. These diseases demand us to center our lives on them. As we run around and around trying to fulfill their neverending desires, we join their sick world by slowly losing our identity. We lose faith in our sense of the truth and we lose confidence in ourselves. We no longer trust in our ability to manage our lives, they do it for us. Living a life that is directed and controlled by someone else is not only demeaning but highly toxic to our system.

What is most confusing is that even though this process of total submission to the *oppressor's* desires is harmful for the victim, it is perceived and demanded by the *oppressor* as an act of being in "love." Therefore, in his belief of what love is, and his assumption for "love" to exist,

your needs must not exist. Whether this makes sense to you or not, it is not relevant to him. That is what he believes, that is what he demands, and he must be "right."

Do not become intimidated and do not fear this abusive individual. Be assured that beneath the mask of total power and delusions of grandeur there is powerless, wounded child tormented by his own insecurity and self-centeredness. Every day, he silently struggles to keep and display his misunderstood sense of power.

Throughout the course of our lives, we may find ourselves falling into the trap of the *oppressor*, the one who insists on taking advantage of others. Whether this *oppressor* is an individual, group, or culture itself, we must realize that we have the power to change and control our lives. Even though we may be driven by forces and circumstances which sometimes might be beyond our control and awareness, we are also the authors of our own fate, our ultimate destiny.

Remember, the freedom to see and be who we truly are is the greatest gift given to us, not by men, but grace. It already belongs to us. We just need to claim it and it is not far away.

The Predator's Prey

I feel like a princess in the top of the castle
My heart is running, the night is coming
And my silent tears are falling,
For there is nothing I can do.

Like in ancient times,
The king has sent his queen to the tower
For her to be destroyed,

For she has disobeyed the king . . .
Actually . . . because he just decided to do so.

Disobedience or not, was never an issue,
Nor was it relevant
To his brutal and cruel instincts.

She was just standing in the way of his desires,
Therefore, she became expendable,
And to get rid of her was his only plan
No feelings, no guilt, and no regret.

We don't need to go to other countries to find mistreated and abused people. We must not read about an abusive relationship and conclude that it describes something happening only in other countries. Not true. The abuse and mistreatment of others is going on at this very moment in our communities. Even though freedom and civil rights are well advertised, they are not always followed or enforced.

The Frog and the Scorpion

The use of metaphors is a simple way to learn and share the wisdom of time. The following metaphor enlightens one's understanding of predatory nature.

The Frog and the Scorpion

There was a scorpion and a frog at the side of a river.
The scorpion asked the frog for a ride across the water.
The scorpion said, "I really would like to get to the other side of this water and it would take me a very long time to walk around the water to get to the other side. If you give me a ride I can get across in a short time."
The frog said, "If I give you a ride you will sting me and I will die."
The scorpion said, "No, I won't sting you because, if I

do, I will fall into the river and die. I really want to get to the other side."

Finally, the frog said, "okay."

So the scorpion got on the back of the frog. Halfway across to the other side, the scorpion stung the frog. The frog looked up at the scorpion and said, "Why did you sting me?! You said you wanted to get to the other side. Now we will both die!"

The scorpion said to the frog, "I really did want to get to the other side and I really didn't mean to sting you."

The frog said, "Why did you sting me then?"

The scorpion said, "Because, it is in my nature."

It is the intention of the scorpion to cross to the other side, but it is also in the nature of the scorpion to sting and kill.

As humans we have been given the right to choose between two intrinsic natural forces within our selves—the power to create and the power to destroy. We have been given the potential for wisdom and the strength to rise above our instincts. But to many distractions and temptations along the path seem to blur our vision, which sidetracks us. We end up drifting away from our purpose in life, and from our true source of power. These distractions are very seductive and appealing to our senses and they seem and feel so good and real that it is difficult to know what is true. Somehow, we end up losing our strength and drifting into the unconscious streams of life, falling into the fabricated illusions of this world again and again. . . .

Well-intentioned messages and good advice seem to come to our rescue, but we often find that a good intention is seldom enough to cross the stream of life with its mass of illusions and distractions along the way. A rude awakening is necessary for our consciousness to begin fiercely fighting for control of our life. An uncompromised burning desire and determination to use our will is necessary to cross the world of illusion in order to attain the long-desired everlasting happiness for which we all yearn.

So, how can you cross the stream of life without being stung by the scorpions—the *oppressors* of life? **Avoid them, if you can!** Remember, it is easier to avoid falling into the traps than it is getting out of them. Now, if you are already trapped; there is a way out. In the following chapters, you will find the information and the tools you require as it relates to your particular situation. You will need to get a firm grip on the *rules of the game* in life as well as the effective strategies to keep you on track. Be assured the win is already yours!

Mother Nature's self-preservation has already given us the tools and skills that we need to get out of the traps. You just need to remember them as you become aware of your own intuitive and instinctive power within you. Many brave souls like you have done it. You are not alone, and you have what it takes to turn it around! That is why you are reading this book. Welcome to a life of passion, joy, and happiness. This is the result of living a congruent life based on a clear and non-conflicted mind and spirit. You **must** believe in yourself.

II
The Battlefield or the Playground?

Know Where You Stand

The Battlefield or the Playground? . . . **Your Choice.**

Whether it is in business or in relationships, whether you have been deceived or not, this is where you are. Perhaps you can still make it fun! In this game, playing it "fair" or doing what is "right" with our opponent, the *oppressor,* is a wasteful battle. He won't play fair and he won't do what is right. Why? Because he doesn't have the capacity to do it, and it would end the game. Total honesty is not part of his game. That would burst the bubble of his egocentric identity. Not only would it be devastating for him, it would not be fun for you either, as it may trigger his anger.

This world can be a wonderful and exciting playground, but you need to play his game with intelligence; or you will be taken out of the game. Whether you know it or not, you have now entered into the game of life. Denying this reality will only hurt you and it will be to your own disadvantage. You have been called to play in this game, and the name of the game is **WIN**.

Please understand that the purpose of this book is not to destroy your perception of love, hope, and beauty in this world. The purpose of this book is not for you to become cynical and deceitful. The purpose of this book is not to destroy your opponent. The purpose of this book is to give you the skills to re-build your strength. The intention of this book is to enable you to successfully navigate and control the direction of your life and destiny. The purpose of this book is for you to understand the nature of your *oppressor,* and to win at his or her game.

The Game of Life
Rules of Engagement

Rule #1   **Protect yourself:** The potential for change is imbedded in human nature. Regardless of how good a person's intentions may be, and in spite of the great promises made, they still may not follow through. <u>Always protect yourself</u>!

Rule #2   **Rule of nature:** Respect the animal kingdom by keeping your distance. We cannot change nature, but we can learn how to live with it. A scorpion can only sting if you are near it. A bee will sting if you provide a challenge. Do not challenge the *oppressor*.

Rule #3   **Know where you stand:** Understand the rules of the game before you play. Assume nothing. Otherwise, the price can be too high—emotionally, financially, and physically.

     a) *Observe and listen.* What are the rules, beliefs and behaviors that sustain the game? What is expected of you? Most important, identify which are the possible pitfalls that can eliminate or replace you from the game. Remember, it is not what your *oppressor* says, it is what he <u>does</u> that counts! Avoid deceiving yourself by

31

believing his excuses. All things move accordingly to their nature. Observe his patterns and his actions.

b) *Never put all of your eggs in one basket.* The nature of life is to change, we are bound by the same natural law and the rules of the game can change without notice. Be prepared, be informed, and educate yourself. Like the old saying goes: "Why light one candle when you can light twenty?" Knowing that the wind is always blowing even when it appears to be steady; it is actually in motion preparing to blow again. Reach out for support and ask for what you need. Prepare yourself.

c) *Anticipate your opponent's move to block and detour you from your good intentions.* His strategy is to sabotage your intention to do better in life by misguiding you on what is "best for you." Find your own way and do not allow him to distract you. Open your eyes and look for possibilities. What can you do to prepare yourself? Even a small window today, can be a big door tomorrow. Remember, as long as you keep faith in yourself, you still have a chance to win the game. Do not give up.

Rule #4   **Know your opponent:** So, you think you cannot beat your opponent? Then join him. What are his strengths? What are his weaknesses? What does he desire? What does he expect from you? Every fortress has its weakness; look for the weak and unprotected road to his fortress by joining him.

Rule #5　**Style of engagement:** You don't really know your opponent until you engage him. What you now know about him is not all there is. Do not assume and never sell him short. Be alert and study him. He will react according to the way you choose to engage and relate to him. Observe his reactions. If your chosen strategy does not get you what you want, then choose another and try again.

Rule #6　**Keep a good sense of humor:** In this game the first one to get mad loses. Anger tends to blind our perception and trigger our impulses. <u>Not a good idea.</u> Besides, it is not good sportsmanship to get angry at your opponent. Remember, your expressions of anger will likely create more anger in your opponent. This is the first step to losing the game. A deep breath and a smile are more efficient. Not reacting to him will help you maintain focus on your goals and preserve what is important to you. Do not get distracted. Keep your eye on the ball.

Identifying the Traps

Life is not about how many times we fall, but how we bounce back and turn it around. There is always a way!

The need for humans to have control is healthy and natural. However, it becomes unhealthy and destructive when we demand *complete* control and impose our desires and arbitrary needs on others for our own personal gain. This is, indeed, a dangerous and destructive process to all involved, including the *oppressor*. It will just be a matter of time for his false power to crumble. Time after time, we have seen how prey, the victims of oppression and abuse, have always found a way to get out of their traps. Throughout history, we have seen how oppression in humans creates resentment and sets the scene for later wars. Be assured of Mother Nature's wisdom, there is no mistake about it. She has already imbedded in the prey's natural instincts the skill to survive and succeed.

Consequently, having a deep understanding and full compassion for our fellow *oppressor,* there is no need to *fear him.* Do not match his fear. Instead, come from a place of love and understanding. Furthermore, your perceived enemy is already wounded. First, his fragile ego makes him dependent on others for praise and reassurance in order to validate his existence. Secondly, in his false sense of superiority and omnipotence his weakness resides. His ego is weak, his structure is fragile, and his fortress is easily penetrable. Nevertheless, in the wilderness of the open forest of life, the word is *caution*. Stay alert and never ever underestimate your opponent.

Therefore, "tell the truth"—"tell it for what it is"—"let go and vent your anger" it is not going to do it—not with this *oppressor*. These techniques are for people whose level of reasoning allows them to think, to reflect on how they choose to participate in life. Consequently, they function and engage in reasonable communication. An *oppressor* is not a creature of reason, but rather a creature of emotion. He functions in a world of emotions by overreacting to small events, and he is not capable of taking responsibility for his own behavior. He fears losing control in a world that he cannot, and must not, trust.

Do you find yourself falling into his trap? You don't need to feel guilty for falling into his trap; we do sooner or later—that is how we learn to survive. Life is a process of learning, there is nothing to be ashamed of. Instead, there is a lot to learn. Besides, the *oppressor* is skillful at what he does, and he is not easily recognized by the untrained naive eye. To identify and recognize the *oppressor* takes time and preparation. Nonetheless, the sooner you learn to identify this *oppressor,* the better you will be. Remember, it is not what life brings to you, but what you do with it that matters!!

Be patient. You are learning and you are in life training. The purpose of being with this *oppressor* is to recognize your inner strength by learning who you truly are. As you lose your naivete, created by past social conditioning, you become stronger and wiser. This is the loss of your unrealistic beliefs and expectations that made you an easy prey for his predations. A loss that is necessary to grow and mature. This allows you to cross this stream of illusions and disbeliefs without losing your strength. Do this with a clear purpose in mind—to get your life under control and live the outstanding life that you deserve

You may wonder why you are unhappy. "Is it dependency?" "Is it loving too much?" or "Is it just fear of being alone?" Whatever the reasons may be, or whatever you have been told they are, the end result is the same. You still need to get out of the trap, and turn your life around. No one else can do it for you. You must do it and you **can** do it!

Remember, life is not about how many times we fall, but how we bounce back and turn it around! Be confident and trust in yourself. There is always a way.

In this chapter you will find practical strategies to increase your instinctive power to master and persuade your opponent. You will learn that your *oppressor* has a false identity and a root core belief that, once understood, will unlock a powerful force within you to open the gate and gracefully defeat him. This will, however, open the door of opportunity for you to become aware and dare to create a masterpiece of your life by learning about yourself and how to control and direct your thoughts and emotions. Finally, you will unfold and become all that you can be. Know that you are not alone; many others are doing it. I am with you on this journey.

Are you feeling trapped? Attend to our instinctive skills for self-preservation.

The following are some of the skills that you can use as they relate to your particular situation:

- Stand still. Observe him. Identify the traps and his luring baits.
- Do not react. Fear him not. Your *oppressor* has no more power than the power you give him. Hold on to your power by not reacting to him. Trust in yourself.
- See it for what it is. Avoid speculation and judgment in any direction. Focus on how to solve it and plan how to successfully get out of it.
- Tailor your strategy. Be attentive—if your chosen strategy does not get you what you want, then try a different one. Stay safe.

In looking at your options, you may consider the following:

a) Before you choose to fight, you must have a plan and prepare yourself.
b) Before you negotiate, you need to put yourself in a position of power.
c) Before you escape, you need to develop an escape plan; perhaps it is better to have this *oppressor* be the one who decides to leave in harmony.
d) Whether you choose to stay, leave, play, or fight, it is your choice and personal responsibility—no one else's.

A word of caution. Dealing with physical abuse or any substance abuse, such as alcohol, drugs or stimulants are beyond the scope of this book. If this is the case for you, or the people around you, I strongly recommend that you consult a professional in this area to assist you.

Identifying the Traps

We can be easily deceived when we are under the influence of powerful emotions such as fear, guilt and anger. That is his game. Observe him.

In order to live with this dominant individual we adapted by repressing our emotions and needs, and by showing only the ones that fit his script. Why? Because he has already declared what our wants and needs "should" and "ought" to be. We had to show "respect" which he often interpreted as "obedience" to his wishes and desires. We had to show "appreciation" in ways that he demanded. In our attempt to meet this person's needs, we began to deny our own perception and feelings, to the point where we dissociated ourselves from reality. We no longer trusted in what we saw, heard, and felt. We no longer knew what we really wanted, because it had already been decided by our *oppressor*. We started drifting down in the slow and deadly path of losing our identity. We ended up feeling confused, and not having a clue to why we feel the way we do.

The following will help you to identify some of the strategies this *oppressor* uses to secure control.

This Oppressor reassures control by:

1. **Intimidation:** He intimidates you with aggressive movements, looks, gestures, and threats to hurt, or abandon you. A hostile tone is commonly used.

2. **Confusion:** He blames you for his feelings because you "don't or won't understand him." The game he plays depends on him being vague and non-specific regarding his wants and needs. Therefore, you are set up to fail because no matter how hard you try, you cannot read his mind. Although, no one can read his mind, yet he blames you for it.

3. **Guilt:** "You don't care for me." "If you cared for me, you would do what I say." "After all that I do for you." "I feel hurt when you don't trust me." By making you feel guilty, he gains control.

4. **Put downs:** You are always wrong and you never measure up to his expectations. He "knows everything" and he is "right." Or after putting you down he claims that he was "just kidding." He uses these hurtful comments to cover up his feelings of shame and incompetence. Therefore, don't take it personally. It has nothing to do with you, he is just responding to his own monologue to reassure himself of his own superiority. Shake it off!

5. **Isolation:** He experiences fear when he sees you talking to other people because he does not want them to give you "bad ideas." He will try to prevent you from improving yourself in ways such as getting a better education or starting your

own business. He does not want to lose control over you.

6. **False accusations:** Whether his accusations are true or false, it does not matter to him. The message he wishes to convey is that "you are not good enough." He will make these arbitrary and unfounded accusations without having evidence to support them.

7. **Financial control:** The more you depend on him financially, the more control he has.

Are you feeling fearful, guilty, or confused? That is precisely the feeling our *oppressor* wants you to have—**it is his trap. Do not fall into it.** We are easily deceived when we are under the influence of powerful emotions, such as fear, guilt, and anger. That is his game. He is trying to move you onto an emotional playing field that is unleveled, where your judgment will be impaired. Consequently, you won't be able to see the evidence before you.

First thing you want to do is not to react. Instead, observe what he does. Do not confront or question his behavior. Just pay close attention by observing him.

Know Your Opponent

In order to defeat your opponent you need to understand him. In order to stop his predations you must persuade him. Most *oppressors* perceive their victims as weak and dependent. His victim is to be unintelligent and unable to make decisions on her own. A victim is an object that he possesses, and her only function is to fulfill and become all that he desires. This individual sees himself as strong, intelligent, competitive, and in control. Pride and vanity are at the top of his priority list. This person is a servant of his or her own desires and you are expected to meet these needs; to nurture, and support this person's idealized and egocentric self-image.

The following are basic strategies that you can use to place you in a position of power while you develop a plan the works for you. Remember, these strategies are not to be used indiscriminately but only to defeat predatory behavior. The purpose is to understand not to deceive your opponent. The objective is to master his self-absorbed world without losing your strength.

How to place yourself in a position of power.

I—Build a Platform of Kindness and Safety
THE DO'S AND DON'TS

<u>DO</u>

- **<u>Disarm him.</u>** Follow the Golden Rule by being kind. An *oppressor* would not destroy one of his own species. It is not in his nature. The objective is to gain his respect and trust by sincerely becoming his best friend. Establish rapport by establishing similarities. You can do this by mirroring him; moving like him, talking like him, being like him; and encourage him to talk about himself and the things he likes most. He will perceive you as one with him and he won't need to fear you anymore.

- **<u>Praise him.</u>** Praise him for anything and everything he does and says. Like most *oppressors,* he has a very fragmented ego. Be sincere when you praise him as his identity is based on his belief of how others perceive him; consequently, he needs constant reassurance of who he thinks he is. Whether his self-perception is true or not, it is true to him and that is all that matters. You should not destroy that image, but seek to keep it and reinforce it. Otherwise, it could be devastating for him, and it may backfire on you. Therefore, assure him that his performance is as successful as what he perceives it to be.

- **<u>Do persuade him.</u>** How? What does he want from you? What is his image of you? Does he see you as a weak, dependent, unintelligent individual? Be attentive to his needs and keep his interest by listening to what he desires. This will keep you close to him and then you will know what his plans are for you. Always be a polite and pleasant ally, not a threat. Once he feels in control this is the time to persuade him into your direction and ask for what you need. This way, you get what you want and he gets what he wants—a win-win situation!

- **Appeal to his kindness and caring instincts** to protect the ones that look like him and are loyal to him. After all your hard work, you deserve it. Make him feel proud of any and all concessions that he makes, including the smallest ones. He bases his existence on what others think of him. He feels superior and he likes others to be dependent on him. This gives him a strong sense of importance. Therefore, present your needs and desire as indirect suggestions so that he thinks it is his decision and not yours.

DO NOT

- **Do not contradict him.** He is not capable of accepting being wrong. An opinion different from his is perceived by him as a threat to his fragile ego, the core of his identity. He needs to be and he must be "always right" and in control. If he pressures you to give him an answer, consider responding in a vague, polite, kind manner.
- **Do not confront him.** He does not take responsibility for his actions. Taking responsibility requires maturity and a process of thinking called reasoning. This is not where he is coming from. Your opponent cannot activate his capacity to reflect on his behavior. Things "just happen to him." Confronting him will only make you a target for his anger. Whenever possible admit that it is your

mistake, even though it is not. This will reinforce the perfect image of himself, and it will destroy any fuss he could create. After all, he does believe you to be unintelligent, and to be dependent on his constant guidance. He will then feel superior and in control which is his driving force.

- **Do not argue.** Do not engage in trivial and wasteful battles by defending yourself. You don't have to prove yourself. Instead, keep your strength and *win* this game by not involving your ego. That is by not proving him wrong. You can do this by respecting his beliefs and showing appreciation for his effort. Please understand that this does not mean that you agree. It means that you just cannot change what he chooses to believe. After all, it is just his opinion.
- **Do not show your weak points.** Do not show your frustration and disappointment as it will only put him on guard whereby he will distrust you. Remember, he expects you to be at one with him, and not different than him. Not that it is right. Not that it makes sense, but that is how his mind functions. He reacts and he attacks everything and everyone that he perceives as different from him.
- **Be careful.** Strive for your safety.

As I mentioned before, dealing with this arbitrary and oppressive individual at any level requires a brave heart, intelligence, and all the help that you can receive from God. I have found the following commandments to be most important to remember and practice.

The Three Commandments for Life

First Commandment: "You Shall Not Adore Anyone but Me."

Do not place the *oppressor* in the place of the Almighty Universal Force. The moment you do so, you are giving him the power to bring you down. Would you give pearls to the pigs? I hope not. Remember that we cannot blame the pigs for destroying the pearls. The pigs don't know any better, because it is in their nature to destroy the pearls. They have no appreciation for them. On the other hand, it is your responsibility to protect and take care of the pearls. In this case, the pearls are *you*. Furthermore, it is not wise to depend totally on someone else to meet your needs. Some people can be as fragile as a figure of clay which is destined to break sooner or later. Trust and fully depend on the unlimited Almighty Force within yourself to feel loved and protected. Be wise.

Second Commandment: "Treat Others the Way You Would Like to Be Treated."

Use the power of love and forgiveness. Once you understand your opponent's self-centeredness which is motivating this behavior, you will forgive them; but also remember their nature. This way, you will be able to recognize and not fall into these traps again. Forgiveness is the attitude of a strong and healthy individual who refuses to engage in the tempting wasteful battles of anger and resentment. Instead, this individual chooses to function at a more powerful, loving, and creative way. There is power in forgiveness . . . Forgive.

Third Commandment: "Never Forget Who You Truly Are."

If things are looking down and you feel tired, just remember who you truly are. You have been given the power to think, the power to create, the power to reason, and the power to choose. This is a gift given to you by grace, not by man. You are made in the image of the Almighty and it is your right and responsibility to function at that level. Re-establish and keep the contact with your true self. Allow the divine wisdom within you to guide you and help you do the job. Call on God's strength to guide you and empower you with what you need to succeed in life. You will be heard and your energy will be restored. You will witness His power. Always remember who you really are.

The freedom to see and be who we truly are is the greatest gift given to us, not by man, but by Grace. It belongs to us by divine and human right. We just need to claim it, and it is not far from us. It is not a dream; it is a reality. To exercise this freedom it takes courage, unselfishness, and the faith of certainty. A wonderful path not walked by the many but the few. It is not an easy path, but well worth living. This path is not only for the "saints," the "pure," or the "chosen," it is also for the brave at heart, like you who commits to rise to the challenge of life which is to live from the depths of your heart and to stand for what truly matters—***you.***

Know Your Weakness

*Under the influence of strong
feelings we are easily deceived.*

—Aristotle

What are you afraid of?

What is causing you to live in fear? What is making you
feel tired, confused, guilty, and depressed? What makes
you think that you have no control over your life? What
untruths have you been told to believe that got you in
trouble? What do you keep telling yourself that keeps you
hopeless? What do you fear most?

Whatever it is that is keeping you in fear is making
you feel hurt and helpless, and it needs to be recognized.
Denying, justifying, or running away from these feelings
will not help you. It will only increase the fear and cause
you more pain. The more you run from it, the bigger it will
get. The sooner you face it, the faster it will disappear. You
need to become aware of what it is and acknowledge it.
Blaming, criticizing, or feeling guilty will only distract
and deplete your energy. What do you really fear? Is it the
fear of failure? Is the fear of being alone? Do you fear for
the sake of your children? Do you fear losing your financial support?

47

Whatever your worst fear is, you need to accept it. Ask yourself: "What is the worst that can happen?" Once you identify your worst fear, look for possible solutions or alternatives. Do not get stuck on *what if's*. Make a plan that works for you and follow it.

When we experience fear our body automatically prepares to protect itself. Ignoring or denying the signals of self-protection, and choosing to remain under the tread of fear, causes a great level of tension which is very harmful to us. This creates physical and emotional pain which can lead us into addictive and compulsive behavior. Why? Because, fear is one of the most highly charged emotions. Once triggered, requires a stronger charged emotion to overcome it. Substance abuse and compulsive behavior gives us a false sense of relief. It only gives us a quick fix to our emotional pain. It is a seductive and downward spiral.

Making matters worse, pharmaceutical corporations perpetuate the illusion of relief by marketing quick-fix medicines. We become dependent on these substances, and we lose control over our lives. Living under fear is not only highly toxic and damaging to our health, but it frequently invites chaos and tragedy.

Remember—nothing is, unless you **think** it is. For anything to exist you must create it and believe it in your mind. The more you believe in your fear, the more weak and vulnerable you become. Whatever beliefs and circumstances might have led you onto the path of pain and sorrow, it is now time to place yourself in a position of power and to regain control of your life. It may be difficult at first, but it is not impossible. It may just take you a little bit longer than you thought. Do not stumble; do not fear! **The worst thing you can do is give up and not try.** Keep your eyes open and hope in your heart—you will find the way.

Rose Mary: A survivor

An attractive and intelligent thirty-four-year-old woman has been married to David for the past seven years. She was a loving wife, and a caring mother of two children, two and five years old. When Rose Mary came to see me, she was feeling severely depressed and hopeless.

Despite taking heavy dosages of psychiatric medication, she continued to feel depressed. She was very confused. She felt guilty for not being a "good" wife. She blamed herself and she believed that the problems in her marriage were all her fault. The more she tried to reason with David, her husband, the more he blamed her for everything. She felt at the bottom of the downward spiral and she feared she was going "crazy." Since Rose Mary loved her husband, it was difficult for her to see his manipulative and abusive behavior. She feared for her future and the well-being of her children as she fully depended on David for financial and emotional support. Once in treatment, Rose Mary joined Victims of Crime Program and received support and education to be in control of her life again. Last time I saw Rose Mary, she was a happy and proud mother who had started a small jewelry business at home. She was excited about her life, and with a smile on her face, she proudly showed me a fine gold chain with two beautiful charms hanging close to her heart. These charms were the figures of two little children—her own children. They gave her the strength and passion to stand on her own, and to fight for her life. Needless to say, Rose Mary did not need more psychiatric medication. Although she was still married to David, they lived in separate homes. David was attending professional counseling.

Place Yourself in a Position of Power

I think, therefore I am.
—Descartes

I—Master Your Beliefs
II—Master Your Emotions

Our beliefs determine how we feel. It is not **what** happens to us but **how** we interpret what happens to us that will determine how we feel and respond to the events of life. Consider this: Pregnancy is an event that may have very different meanings for women. The meaning they will associate with it is in direct relationship to what they associate with pregnancy. If a woman believes that being pregnant is a blessing, she will feel happy. If she believes that being pregnant will interrupt her plans in life, she will feel unhappy. The event is the same—her response is based on what it means to her.

Our beliefs have the incredible power to bring us up or down in life. Exploring our beliefs is a journey on its own. It can take a long time, but it could greatly enhance your life. For the ones who need to make fast changes in their lives this book will offer shortcuts to increase control of their life by realizing the effects of their emotions. This will be done by identifying the benefit and damage from experiencing a specific emotion, and deciding what emotion is in your best interest to help you obtain what you want in life. For example: How will it help or hurt you to be angry? What are the positive and negative consequences of feeling depressed? What is anger and resentment doing to you? Does feeling angry help you to get what you want? If you decide that feeling angry is not in your best interest, then you must focus your attention on the emotion that you want to experience, such as acceptance, joy, or happiness, which will help you accomplish what you desire.

Our authentic power and freedom reside in our ability to choose responsibly how to think by ourselves, and make our own decisions. It is not that we have no control of our lives; we simply do not take the time to stop and think what is in our best interest. Consequently, we tend to react impulsively by experiencing and expressing emotions that are often harmful to ourselves and others. It is an illusion to believe that life, and the way we feel, is not in our control.

We place ourselves in power by choosing to experience positive emotions that are going to give us a powerful emotional state, a feeling of well-being, such as love, self-acceptance, and trust. When we do this, we feel strong, happy and excited about life. On the other hand, the impulse toward anger, hate, and resentment will only hurt you, leaving you tired and weak. These negative emotions are seductive and impulsive. They tend to get our life out of control. Remember, negative thoughts will lead us into negative actions.

Therefore, we must choose our thoughts very carefully, as they are the seed of every action and feeling that we have. If you change your thoughts and expectations of where you are in life, or what you may expect from yourself or others, you will change your feelings about it. For instance, if you think that you are "not good enough" you are going to feel sad, frustrated, and angry. If you choose to think that you are "good enough" and that you appreciate yourself, then you will feel good about yourself. You will feel loved and confident in yourself to direct your life.

This is indeed, the most powerful shift of energy—**self-acceptance and self-approval. You are good enough to be loved and respected.** This is your birthright and, it has the power to reject the false images that you have believed about yourself. You **don't** have to be at the mercy of negative thoughts and fearful feelings that sneak up on you and make your life miserable.

You **do** have a choice. Take charge of your life by taking control of your thoughts and feelings.

As we face and experience the power of our divine nature, the unlimited potential that we have, we use our creative mind to focus on and manifest what we truly want in life. We do this by choosing our beliefs and experiences in life. It is our privilege and personal responsibility to decide how we will shape and color our life, our destiny. Remember, everything could be taken away from you, except your inner strength. Only you can give up your soul. **Do not give your power away!**

It is a fact that we cannot change our past, neither can we predict our future, but we can prepare and succeed in life. As you prepare, you begin at this very moment to increase your power by practicing the following steps:

1. Refuse to entertain any thoughts and feelings that weaken and deplete your strength. Negative thoughts are intended to make you feel weak and hopeless. They are like thieves, waiting for the opportunity to sneak in and rob your life energy. As

justified as these emotions seem to be, and as painful as they are; they just don't help! They are too costly and totally drain your energy to the point of becoming lethal to your health. You need to step out of these thoughts and shift to positive ones. They will only be dissolved by acknowledging the negative effects they have on your life.

POWERLESS THOUGHTS (Negative—Low Frequency)	POWERFUL THOUGHTS (Positive—High Frequency)
Fear	Trust
Hopelessness	Acceptance
Anger	Compassion
Resentment	Forgiveness
Hate	Love
Guilt	Responsibility
Shame	Self-Acceptance
Emptiness	Purpose
Hopelessness	Hope
Self-Doubt	Certainty

As you focus your mind on powerful thoughts, you will become more confident and stronger. You may do this by taking time to write down some of your good qualities and repeat those to yourself every day as you reflect on them, i.e. "I love myself," "I am good enough." If you like to sing, sing! Singing helps to keep negative thoughts away, and your spirit high. Stay away from people who insist on playing their songs of resentment, anger, and envy. When they say, "There's nothing to be happy about," and when they criticize you or put you down—just smile, take a deep breath, and *sing your song of love anyway!* This is your life. You own and create every single moment. No one has the right to destroy your happiness and no one can. Keep your power.

> *See what you see*
> *Hear what you hear*
> *Avoid any and all speculation*
> *Make no judgment . . . stand still*

2. Refuse to entertain any and all beliefs that decrease your self-confidence, such as believing that you are "not worth it" and that you "don't have what it takes." Those negative beliefs are intended to confuse you, to make you feel weak, and helpless. The following are some suggestions to increase your awareness and strength:

   a) Sharpen your senses—**observe.** Do not get confused. Actions speak louder. It is not what the *oppressor says or dictates* that is important, but what you choose to believe.

   b) Be attentive to what you see. Do not justify his behavior.

   c) Trust in your intuitive sense. Trust in yourself.

3. Do Not Fear. Fear paralyzes our reasoning. Acknowledge your worst fear and overcome it. Your fear is based on your misperception that he has all the power to give or withhold what you need. The fact is that he may have some of the power—but he does **not** have the absolute power to meet all your needs. No one does and no one can. On the other hand, you have all the potential and power to meet those needs better than anyone. **You can do it.**

4. Stop believing that you have no way out. This creates a feeling of fear and hopelessness. It leaves you tired, fatigued, and powerless. It increases your opponent's control over you. That is exactly what he wants. Step out of it! You are not in a hopeless trap—it is temporary. You are in life's training.

5. Are you mad now? Realize you are only hurting yourself and he is getting his way. By allowing him to upset you, he is controlling your emotions; and therefore, controlling you. Observe him, do not react. As a wise and courageous woman said, "Thank God, wings were not given to scorpions as they can only sting you while you are on the ground." Be smart. Stay off the ground by not reacting to him.

6. Feeling down because you are not good enough? The fact that he does not acknowledge how important and valuable you are, does not mean that you are not worth it. Don't fall for it. He is not capable of being sensitive to your wants and needs, and he lacks the ability to express empathy. This is one of his mental and emotional handicaps. Would it be realistic for you to expect a crippled individual to walk straight? Of course not. In order to keep ourselves in power it is important to have realistic expectations. Therefore, stop expecting what he can not give.

7. Do you believe that you have failed? You have not failed. There is no failure in life if you learn.

You are learning one of the most painful lessons in life. You are taking off the rose-colored glasses to see the real world. You are losing your naiveté as you become stronger and more mature. This is an opportunity to learn and do things more intelligently. Therefore, there is no failure, but merely gains. You have a brave heart and you will succeed.

8. Should you forgive? To forgive is not a sign of weakness. It is a sign of strength. You forgive because you refuse to carry the heavy baggage of resentment. When you choose not to forgive, you choose to carry the hate and resentment which will contaminate and ultimately poison your life.

Why does he need to hurt you? Because, it is in his nature to react and sting anybody he can. Why? Because, he is programmed to do so. He is wired that way. You may be asking: Can I change him? Can I kiss the frog and turn him into the prince? The answer lies in you. Chapters II and III describe the steps to help you build your strength and shift things around. Chapter IV will assist you in using the ultimate power of transformation should you decide to embrace such a noble quest and try to persuade him to change. At that time, it will be important that you carefully assess your particular circumstances and your opponent's degree of dysfunction. Emotional abuse is not to be justified or overlooked. You may also consider consulting with a professional to help you asses the level of risk and alternatives. Remember, we cannot change anyone. We can only persuade them in our direction.

Never Underestimate Your Opponent

Never underestimate your opponent. Most battles have been lost by assuming all is well and getting too comfortable. Remember, the nature of your opponent is very emotional. Therefore, he is susceptible to abrupt change whether you trigger him or not. The following suggestions will help you stay alert and on top of the game.

1. Keep your attention on your opponent by observing his actions and protecting yourself. His perception of reality can be easily distorted by his negative self-talk which can trigger a vicious defense reaction against you. Be prepared. Keep your documents and records safe.

2. Keep yourself close to your opponent. Do this by being polite and pleasant to him. Because of his conflictive mind and his emotional instability, it is important that you know what is on his mind. Do not assume what he will do or say. Never sell him short.

3. If you are ever in trouble because you disobeyed his arbitrary orders, apologize immediately. Present it as if it was not your intention to do so. Human tendency is to give the benefit of the

doubt. You may consider using this benefit to avoid unnecessary conflict.

4. Do not admit your plan or success. As tempting as this could be, do not admit it. This could trigger his competitive nature against you. Present your victory as matter of luck or just an accident. Such as by simply stating that "it just happened."

5. Do not confront him. By nature, your opponent cannot deal with the truth. His perception is limited and narrow. Be kind and understand his intrinsic limitations. Besides, confrontation can be very unpleasant for you. Life has its own way of bringing enemies; we do not need to create more.

6. If in danger, listen to your basic instincts for self-preservation. Do not deny; do not justify his behavior. Reach out and ask for help immediately. **Always protect yourself!**

III
Awakening Your Inner Strength

Beyond Social Conditioning

Monkey see—monkey do.

How can we succeed in an uncertain and at times deceitful world without becoming cynical and resentful? How can we keep our integrity and moral principles? How do we succeed without losing what truly matters in life?

As our society keeps promising happiness at the end of the road, we obediently respond to the given model of material success. We accumulate many possessions, degrees, and positions of power to prove to others that we are succeeding. If we refuse to follow this model of success, we are perceived as failures.

As we pursue this model of happiness through the achievement of material success, we often find that we were chasing an illusion. We were running east looking for a sunset.

The more we run, the farther away we get from achieving happiness. The more material things we accumulate, the more we want. Soon, we become ashamed of ourselves, as we cannot possess the symbols of success dictated by our society. Feeling shame for "not being good enough" to succeed in this society keeps us running in a fearful and endless circle. This is a catch-22 situation where you are "damned if you do, damned if you don't."

As our society becomes more materialistic, our personal wants and needs become more artificial; and our so-

61

cial rules and roles become more confused. The common statements of "everybody does it," and "who cares," tend to prevail and drive our lives. We are left with the persuasion of the corporate controlled media, a specific book, or the doctor's advice of how to do it "right." As we strive to do our best, we often find ourselves struggling harder. We learn more about the "right" way to be in relationships, which frequently justifies us to end them sooner, or not to start them at all.

We learn all the "right" concepts and theories; yet, we end up with more broken families. Perhaps we are relying too much in our intellect and the "right" way to do it. perhaps it is time for us to stop following what the experts say, and to start trusting our own intuitive wisdom to direct our life.

We are not to surrender to a compliant society in which everything goes and nobody cares. In the name of flexibility and relativity, it is easy to complain and take no accountability for our actions. We are not to become a fearful and fragmented culture in which its wounded children indulge and hide in self-pity, hate, and blame.

We need to take charge of our lives and we must not allow others to decide for us. Now, the time calls for the awakening and reviving of our inner strength. Take charge! Make it happen! Embrace change and master a new mindset of skills and strategies for coping with these most challenging times.

We must choose our own values and beliefs. We must stand for what is deep in our hearts and truly matters in order to impact the lives of our families. Make contact with your inner strength and wisdom. Take immediate control of your destiny.

Do not blindly rely on others for your happiness and success. Indeed, this is your own responsibility. Your power resides right here—right now. Consciously use your mind to make decisions on your own. Open your eyes and realize the power you have. Our potential for reasoning prevents us from becoming complacent vegetables in an already complacent society.

In taking this responsibility, we become determined and committed to succeed in life. Taking control of our life is our right and privilege. It enables us to protect and defend ourselves from the ones who want to take advantage of us. This is why we have eyes to see, ears to hear, and a mind to reason. It is our duty to lead, guide, and protect our children and family from those that insist upon subjecting others to their ignorance and self-centered desires.

We can choose to create and achieve our own model for real success and choose not to follow a deceitful and fragmented model. We do this when we stand for what is right as it benefits all involved, not the few or the one. Whether the *oppressor* is an individual, group or a culture itself who dictates what to do or what to wear, it is our responsibility and human right to wake up from the dream of social conditioning, that is monkey see, and monkey do.

Sense of Purpose

Everything can be taken away from me—But they can never take away my soul, my mind, my spirit.

Every woman has been called to be a leader. This is why the miracle of giving birth has been awarded to her. Her attention to detail, her capacity to nurture, and her ability to focus on multiple tasks are a few of the characteristics that make her sensitive to the unknown. Her intuitive self, the ancient wisdom within, is deeply embedded in her. It continues to compel the human race to evolve and transcend. She is to guide others so they can successfully navigate through life. She is not to be abused or forced to live in darkness and fear. She is to be allowed to freely move and dance. She is to be allowed to freely see, hear, feel, touch, and sense the essence of life without the fear of retribution.

How do we expect women to teach and prepare our children who are the leaders of tomorrow, if we do not acknowledge and support them? How can women lead others when they are expected to repress their feelings, pretend happiness, and unwillingly obey their *oppressor* for the sake of their children? If this be the case, what is then left of her? She is left with nothing but a deep sorrow and a longing to return *home* where she will rest forever.

In addition making things more difficult, women are also called to participate in the corporate world where she is torn between her conflicting roles at home and in society. What a challenge!

However, women have an incredible resilience. Throughout history, they have proven to be natural leaders. They have guarded and guided our families who are the center of our society. Women's maternal instinct to care and protect others has assured our survival. This instinct creates a healthy bond which is necessary for the wellness of the offspring. Women are known to be loyal and hardworking when they are loved and appreciated. They will howl and fiercely fight to protect their nest.

This natural instinct has driven women to dedicate their lives to the wellness of our families. They are the true leaders. They are the ones who strive to see that the needs of the family are met first, and not their own. By their loving efforts and commitment, our families have prevailed and paved the way for the unfolding of our society.

Nevertheless, as women participate more in the corporate world, there is a price to pay. The price is often the destruction of the family unit. It is time to acknowledge the consequence of this movement in society. As women spend more time working, they spend less time with their children. Although there are more material goods at home our children are left without positive role models. Children are now influenced by "TV Mom." This substitute model often carries image of violence, sexual promiscuity, disrespect and vulgarity to our homes. This has a negative and disruptive impact on the minds of our children and our society.

As the family structure continues to be weakened, our children are becoming less savvy. They are not being prepared to deal with the real world, but are misled and misinformed. Therefore, they become easy victims for predatory behavior. Our system is failing as we have more broken families, a decay in moral values, and increase in violence.

These symptoms of our crumbling society are a cry-out call for our roots to be awakened. The speed of change is too fast to keep using the same unsuccessful strategies for coping with life. By denying this reality, we place ourselves on a dangerous path. We have the gift of reason and eyes to see the truth to guide our children and families. We can help to make this a better world.

I am not suggesting that you leave your relationship, change your job, or move to another place; however, I am suggesting that you decide and define your priorities for yourself.

After a long time of living a life of pleasing others and ignoring what we really need and desire, our life energy is depleted. Consequently, we become physically and emotionally sick, and we end up more confused. Furthermore, we lose the connection with our true self.

What is your purpose in life? Why are you here? What do you really want out of life, and why? What are your reasons for living? What makes you feel alive? Listen and believe in yourself. You will find the way by holding on to your passion which is your purpose in life. You are not alone. Remember **you** have the power to influence and create your future.

The freedom to see and be who we truly are is our greatest gift given to us. It takes courage, unselfishness, and the faith of certainty to exercise the gift of freedom. Remember, courage is taking action in the face of fear. Courage is the certainty that our beliefs and convictions are more important than fear. Our convictions mean nothing if we don't take a stand and act on them. In holding on to our convictions and acting on them, we find our power to create what we want in life. You must commit to connecting with yourself and re-establishing your sense of purpose in life.

Make a Plan that Works for You

*The decisions you make to-
day will influence and determine your life tomorrow.*

In order to succeed in life, we must be clear in what we
want and we must develop a plan which will give us what
we want. This plan will include our goals and the steps
that will be taken to succeed.

As we grow and mature, our perception and understanding of this world changes.

Our direction and priorities in life become clear. A
new sense of freedom unfolds and our personal power is
awakened to live a life by our own design. We realize that
the decisions that we have made in the past are not forever. Some of these decisions were based on unrealistic
expectations. Consequently, our life is unfulfilled. As a result, we need to reassess our life and make a more realistic plan. It is important that we develop this plan of action
with specific steps to follow, as it will give you a new sense
of direction and strength. We cannot get to a different destination if we don't have a road map. What are your goals
in life? What would you like to see happen?

Imagine life as a canvas on which you paint. You decide what to paint. You choose the colors that **you** want to
permeate your life with, the ones that **you** dare to live.
This is the plan for your painting, the plan for your life.

As we learned to depend on others for our physical and emotional needs, we find that these expectations are not always fulfilled. As a matter of fact they are seldom fulfilled; leaving us feeling cheated and betrayed. We realize that our dream is not going to come true. Why? Because, the needs of the people we depend on may come first, or they may be incapable of being sensitive to our needs. Do you think this is not fair? Life is not fair! Fairness is a concept. Therefore, it is subjective to personal interpretation. It depends on what a person believes. What is fair to you may not be fair for them, and vice-versa. People do not do what they are expected to do, but what they want to do.

One of the most difficult transitions in life is striving for independence, as it requires us to examine the ways in which we are dependent on others emotionally and financially. If we depend on others to feel loved and appreciated, we need to realize that our cup will not always be full. They may not have the ability or the capacity to fulfill our emotional needs. This is why we need to learn how to love and take care of ourselves. By doing so, our cup will always be full. If we are financially dependent, we need to work toward becoming independent financially by preparing ourselves; whether it means attending school, starting a business, or investing. Even though someone, somewhere, someday may come along to take care of us; it is wise to prepare ourselves for independence. Keep in mind, our happiness and wellness is ultimately our own responsibility.

The following are some steps to be considered as you create your plan for success:

1. **Establish rapport by expressing:**
   a) Physical and emotional similarities

    b) Immediate agreement

2. **Plan your strategy:**
   a) Join your opponent while placing yourself in a position of power.
   b) Learn to manage your emotions. Choose powerful ones.
   c) Make a plan to educate and prepare yourself.

3. **Maintain a deep understanding of the emotional dynamics being played:**
   a) Participate in the game with intelligence. Follow your plan for success.
   b) Prepare yourself to stay, or exit safely, if you choose to leave.

4. **Be clear in what you want.**
   a) Keep your mind focused on your goals. Maintain your balance and strength by protecting and taking care of yourself.

You may be wondering, "Will he ever change?" "Once he looked like a prince, he sounded like a prince, but is he a prince?" Feeling ambivalent is a common experience in life. The decision to stay or leave a relationship is a personal one. It is up to you to take the risk on your own behalf. However, it is also your choice to remain "secure" and not to disturb your emotional and financial stability. Whatever your choice may be at this moment in time, you are no longer a victim. You do have options in life. You must not settle for less than what you can be.

Whatever you do, do not allow anyone to decide for you. The courage to make our own decisions in life is an attribute of a strong and healthy individual. Sometimes we don't need to change our situation; at times, all we need to do is to change our beliefs and strategies so we can successfully cope with life.

As you create your plan for success, it is important to identify your goals and the steps you will take. Be specific in setting your goals and the time frame to achieve them. This will help you stay on course and achieve your goals. Keep in mind that even the smallest step taken today can make a big difference tomorrow. Look for role models around you. Who do you admire? Who is doing what you would like to do? How did they do it? Reach out and ask for support. This may be a good friend, group or helping organization. Perhaps, consider professional advice. The base for success is persitence. Quitting is not an option. Remember, your true happiness is at stake. Plan it and make it happen. It works!

Focus—Keep Your Eye on the Ball

Most games have been lost by getting too comfortable, distracted or confused. It is the intention of your opponent to get you out of balance by controlling the way you feel. He controls your life and emotional state by making you feel sad, fearful, angry, or confused. To counterbalance his intentions you must keep your mind focused on your goals and strategies. It is important to remain clear on what you want. What do you want? What do you want to see accomplished? If your dreams came true, how would your life be different?

Take a moment to imagine. Visualize what you truly want and where you want to be. Create a wonderful thought, a burning desire to see it manifested. Once created in your mind you need to believe in it with absolute conviction. There is no place for doubt. You give power to these thoughts by thinking and focusing on them every day. This is how you will gain strength. Remember, nothing is until you think it is.

Use the power of your imagination to re-focus and to add to these images a strong desire to see them accomplished. The ability to focus your mind will bolster your personal power as you connect with the energy of creation.

Because of our natural tendency to take care of the needs of others, we must avoid attending to all requests arbitrarily. Select, and carefully reflect on the advice and requests received. They can be done with good intention but could be distracting for you; therefore, they could sabotage your goals. Re-focus!

Keep your internal self-talk positive. You may do this by daily stating positive affirmations i.e., "I believe in myself," "I can do it." Remember, positive thoughts lead to positive actions. Moreover, the power and control of your thoughts and feelings are within you. Do not allow fearful thoughts and negative images to weaken your power and detour you from your intent.

The following strategies will help you to stay on course.

1. Observe—Do not react.
2. Study your opponent. Use your chosen strategies.
3. Focus your mind on experiencing positive thoughts and feelings.
4. Create a plan that works for you and follow it. You will succeed.
5. Nurture and believe in yourself. Commit and be determined. Walk with confidence.

Support and Self-Nurturing

Living or dealing with someone who functions at an abusive level can totally drain our energy. This requires us to constantly work on restoring our balance. Understanding and sharing our feelings is not enough for complete healing. We need to become self-nurturing.

This is done by making ourselves feel loved and appreciated. We start by believing in ourselves and by treating us the way we would treat our best friend. We no longer depend or wait on someone to fulfill our needs. As we begin attending to our needs, our energy is restored. Self-nurturing is crucial to our strength as we navigate life.

In order to make contact with our intuitive wisdom, it is important to retreat to take time for ourselves. Remember, no one else can make you happy. Our source of happiness and well-being is not inside others, it is only within ourselves. This is where we need to center our attention and cease looking elsewhere. We need to stop seeking for approval and validation from others. Although it would be desirable to have the love and approval of others, it is not an absolute need. Furthermore, it would be completely unrealistic. No matter how good we are, there will always be someone, somewhere, someplace, that will not approve of us. Why? Because, we are different.

Be aware that taking care of yourself may be threatening for your opponent, as he will not feel needed. Do it anyway! Use his perception of you as a weak and dependent individual to excuse and justify your need to take the time to nurture yourself.

Although our relationships with friends, family, and life-partners are important, they cannot be our absolute source of love. As they are limited by design, they will not always be available. This is why we need to create and depend on our own source of happiness.

Love is an unlimited and unconditional source of energy. It can only be experienced by giving. Do not deprive yourself of it! Stop waiting for others to love you first. Start *giving to you* by nurturing yourself and doing things that make you feel loved and appreciated. Fill up your love tank of energy and you will find yourself giving more love to others.

The Garden

I like to think of life as a garden. In creating your garden, this is what you do:

1. **Select the area where you will plant your garden.** Make your own decisions in life.

2. **Prepare the soil by removing all weeds and stones.** Prepare your mind by removing all negative thoughts and feelings.

3. **Protect your garden from the animal kingdom by building a fence around it. They do not appreciate or respect the flowers.** Protect your peace of mind by setting and demonstrating healthy boundaries.

4. **In your garden, plant and cultivate flowers of your choice. Choose the most beautiful and strongest flowers.** Plant and cultivate positive thoughts and feelings. Chose the most powerful ones.

5. **Water your flowers daily. Do not depend on others to water your flowers as they may forget and your flowers will die. This is your garden.** Nurture yourself daily. Do not depend on others to nurture you as they may not do so and your spirit will despair.

By nature women are driven to love and take care of others. This sometimes leads us into the superwoman syndrome. The more we do, the more we are expected to do. We end up feeling tired and overwhelmed with no time for ourselves. It is appropriate to take time and nurture ourselves. Even the Christian ethics of loving others as yourself assumes that you will provide for your needs first, before you give to others.

Even though, people may ask you for what they desire; it does not mean that you should provide it. Don't get sucked into the *guilt trip*. There are many ways to be polite, and still say NO.

The following are some suggestions to help you keep your balance and prevent fatigue.

- Prioritize. Do things in order of their importance.
- Delegate. Distribute responsibilities.
- Supervise. Encourage and allow others to take care of their needs. Acknowledge their creativity with words of encouragement and guide them.
- Manage your time. Plan the time to nurture yourself. Do not say "yes" immediately. Ask yourself how much time you want to give or spend with that person. You are important, therefore, your time is important, too.
- Set your boundaries. Identify and communicate your wants and needs. It is okay to say no.

It is also important to develop new sources of support and appreciation. It is essential that we acknowledge our need for belonging by reaching out and surrounding ourselves with positive people. Look around and find this support.

The following are some examples to nurture yourself:

- Go for a walk just for the pleasure of it with no destination in mind.
- Take ten deep breaths as you contemplate your surroundings.
- Treat yourself to a nice dinner.
- Treat yourself to massage.
- Play your favorite music.
- Reconnect with a friend that you have lost touch with.
- Exercise. Stretch or do yoga.
- Bake cookies just for yourself.
- Meditate or pray.

- Wander through a bookstore.
- Play with an animal.
- Take a bubble bath—set the candles!
- Write in a diary.
- Take a vacation.
- Buy yourself a present.
- Sing, dance.
- Be creative. What will make you feel loved and appreciated? What would make you come alive? Just Do it!

IV
Manifesting Your True Power

Love—The Power of Transformation

Bless your enemy and you will rob him of his power.
Though many have tried to hunt her.
They all have failed.
Their arrows have transformed into blessings
As she continues to travel free through
The wilderness of the open forest of life.
She finds herself nesting and recreating self
In the Force of the vast Universe
Always transforming, always becoming.
                                                   —Author

To take control of our lives we must learn better ways of coping with life. In order to create and manifest what we want in life we must develop and practice a new mindset. A new mind of powerful thinking where our intentions and actions are clear and congruent; leaving no room for doubt. This mindset comes with the certainty of doing what is right and is in the best interest of all.

Love

Much has been said and written about the power of love. Nevertheless, few have chosen to use it. Love is often interpreted as weak and sentimental; nothing can be further from the truth. Love is not weak. Love is not a sensation. Love is not relative to the selfish and particular desires of an individual. Love is strong. Love is creative. Love is responsibility.

Love is the most powerful energy we can use to transform ourselves and the lives of others, including our enemies.

Love is the highest level of energy in which we can function in our life. It is the result of a conscious and responsible decision to become an active participant in the dynamic field of love. This requires practice and discipline. In order to align ourselves with the powerful energy of love we must let go of our unproductive patterns of beliefs and behaviors that prevent us from living a creative and fulfilled life.

In this chapter, you will find the steps to remove these unproductive patterns which will set you free. You will step into the power of transformation—the energy of *love*. Remember, love cannot be contained. It can only be shared. The more you function and share the dynamic energy of love, the more you will experience the effects of its energy in your life. You will see miraculous results.

Steve: A true leader.

Steve was an intelligent, middle-aged man in his early fifties. He lived with Sarah, his wife, and their four children. Steve was a successful businessman, a leader in his community, and a Master 33 in a respected Masonic Lodge, which is a high-spiritual achievement. Sarah was a devoted wife and dedicated mother who strived to be successful in her marriage.

When Sarah came to see me she was feeling tired, fa-

tigued, and had trouble sleeping. She could not compre-
hend why she was feeling so sad and broke into tears. She
feared not being a "good wife and mother" as she was un-
able to meet the demands of her husband. Steve was a
bright man who "always" knew what was "right" and rep-
rimanded Sarah and the children every time they made a
mistake; almost every day.

Sarah loved her husband she wanted to make him
happy. When I met Steve, he had no awareness of the nega-
tive impact of his behavior on his wife and children. Steve
believed that the way he treated them was in their best in-
terest. Steve's intent was good. The method he used was
not. In his effort to succeed, to be a good husband and fa-
ther, he became abusive to Sarah and the children by putt-
ing them down and demanding perfection. He
disregarded their needs and how they felt. By the end of
session, Steve had reflected on his behavior, and the effect
it had on his wife and children. He realized the great op-
portunity and responsibility that he had taken by becom-
ing a father, the leader of four wonderful children, and a
respectful Master 33 in his community. Now, it was time
for Steve to become a true leader. It was time for Steve to
listen to the needs of others, not to lecture or reprimand. It
was time for him to live and teach others by example, not
by the book or concepts. It was time for Steve to trust in his
inner wisdom to lead.

When I saw Sarah again, she was as happy as anyone
could be. With a big smile on her face she said, "It's like
magic!" Her life and family had turned around. She now
had the strong and loving *Prince* at home again. The man
she once knew.

Reflections

And every time along the path, when I was
Threatened and intimidated by the dark forces
Carried by my ignorant brothers along the path
I paused; I kneeled down; and . . . I prayed.

For it is true, although at times I was exhausted,
I never gave up—and in my tears and pain, I stood still
I then gave thanks for I finally saw . . . the Power of
Transformation, the Power of Love!

Wherever the *predator* is, she is. She is the only one who masters his predations and places him where he belongs. For there she speaks the language of Love—the Power of Transformation.

See It for What It Is

Life is the way it is. Things are the way they are. They are not what we would like them to be, should be, or expect them to be. We have been conditioned to believe and expect that life and people are predictable. We grew up with an illusion of having complete control of our lives.

The truth is that life is uncertain and that we cannot avoid the risks of life. We can only reduce the level of risk. The truth is that people will do what they want to do. Not what we expect them to do. We cannot control them. We can only persuade them in our direction. It does not matter whether this is right or not. This is the way it is. We can acknowledge this reality now and use it for our benefit. Or we can deny it and deal with the consequences later.

If we choose to deny our reality by not attending to the facts of life, we will be spinning inside a hot balloon, waiting for it to explode at any time. This fabricated illusion is not only harmful to us; it is harmful to those around us. The power of "seeing it for what it is" lies in the fact that we can then **do** something about it based on our realistic observations. Not clouded by the way we think they "should be."

When we are willing to accept "what is" we are willing to accept what we see without being judgmental. We then stop wasting time in justifying, complaining, and blaming others. Instead, we place ourselves in a state of inner peace which allows us to clearly see our priorities and to make the necessary changes in our lives. As a result, we no longer focus on feelings of anger, resentment, or guilt. We are free to use our creative minds to manifest what we want in life. **We are free to see.**

Forgiveness

You may be wondering, "If I forgive, would I have to give up my story of being a victim?" "If I give up my story, what would I then have left? After all, I am a victim." No doubt you have been a victim. In some respect, we are all victims of our circumstances. However, by prolonging the "victim state," we fuel the vicious cycle of hate, anger, and resentment. We do not need these emotional traps and powerless feelings.

We need to love and do what is best for ourselves. It is time to acknowledge that these wounds have made you stronger, and they now need to be healed. Not that what happened to you is okay. Not that it was right. But there is time in our life when we need to move on. We need to come to terms with it and do what is necessary to bring closure. This may not be easy to do. However, you deserve to be happy.

There are many reasons to be angry and hurt, but it doesn't help. We need to find reasons to move on. We need to realize what anger and resentment are doing to us. What are we getting from it? How are they holding us back from living? If we want to be happy and become the best that we can be, we need to let go of our wounded memories. We must believe in ourselves and forgive others. If we do not, our wounds will keep the dark cover of fear and pain all over us. This will prevent us from daring to live the life that we deserve—the life that we were meant to live. **There is power in forgiveness. Forgive!**

When we choose not to forgive, it is like wearing dark glasses every day forcing you to see the world this way. Only you—no one else—can envision it that way. By doing this, you end up feeling lonely and you resent others for not feeling like you do. You refuse to live life by keeping yourself trapped in the past—the dark prison of hate and resentment that darkly colors your life.

Forgiveness is the attitude of a strong and healthy individual who refuses to engage in the wasteful battles of anger and resentment. Instead he chooses to function at a more powerful and loving way by forgiving.

We cannot change the past but we can certainly change the way we feel about it. Whatever we have done or has been done to us, we must come to closure. We must come to peace with it. As painful as it might be, we have learned from these experiences. We do not need to carry this pain or cross to prove to others that we are carrying it. The "cross" that we now carry is the "cross" of love which is the true compassion and deep understanding of the intrinsic limitations of human nature.

Feeling pain or joy in life is our personal responsibility. It is our choice. If we choose to continue focusing on our past wounds, we will only re-experience the pain. This pain will continue holding us in the past—we are trapped again! It is in nature for the strongest to survive. It is through suffering that we grow stronger. Wounds are made to be healed. They are not to be kept open and carried around. Allow yourself to heal.

We gain control of our life when we forgive and we choose to focus on the present. Our mind is free, our intention is clear, and our faith is strong. We have no doubts—just the powerful feeling of certainty. This is *the power of love.*

The power of love comes from understanding the nature of your opponent—man or woman—which enables you to disengage and not react to their primitive and irrational level of functioning. Instead, you choose to forgive them, because you understand their inability to function at a higher level of reasoning. They are sadly caught in their own prison of ignorance.

Remember, true happiness has nothing to do with excitement. True happiness is freedom—freedom from all the conditioning of our culture; freedom that allows us to really be ourselves; freedom that comes with the mastery of our emotions so we can direct our lives; the freedom to choose and act accordingly with valid universal principles; not personal, self-centered desires.

My freedom to see, to feel, to think—
My freedom to express myself without fear—
My freedom to choose and do what is right—
My freedom to rise above my basic instincts—
My freedom to design and live the life I deserve.

Will you choose to claim what belongs to you by birth-right? Will you choose to stand up and do what you know is right? Will you choose to unfold your true essence, and achieve ultimate success and everlasting happiness?

We already possess the power to think and make a difference in our lives and in the lives of others. This is our divine right. With this right comes a true sense of power and personal responsibility.

Therefore, we must carefully watch our thoughts and expectations. Every time we react to our perceived "enemy," we add to our fear. Fear him not. He is no match for you. Choose the power of *love*, and you will rob him of his power. Remember, your *oppressor* has only the power you give him. Even if you are currently in a position of total dependency, you **can** turn it around. "Where there is a will, there is a way." The wheel has already been invented. Many others, like you, have done it, and **you** can certainly do it, too. Reach out, educate, and prepare yourself. There is so much waiting for you. All you need is to **believe in yourself.**

What we need to design and master our lives has already been given to us. We must have faith and trust in ourselves. We **do** have what it takes. No doubt about it. This is the fabric of creation that we are to embody. Denying our true essence is detrimental to us. We can run and hide in our busyness by having "no time," being "too tired," and having a "who cares" attitude; but we cannot escape.

As we have learned to fear the unknown, we have also learned not to think on our own, but to follow. We have learned to obey and not question, to assume and not reason. We emulate safety models and we slowly lose our true identity. We follow the trends and we follow the masses. Consequently, we stop taking risks in life. We sadly settle for less in life.

Our longing to return to our source of true power is evident. We are meant to ascend, to rise above our basic instincts and no longer fear. We are to overcome the seductive and well-justified temptations on the road. Whether our *oppressor* is an individual, group, or culture itself, we must take control of our own beliefs and values. We must design and live our lives by keeping our commitment to what truly matters—to dare living our divine lives which we are meant to live. Rise! Seek to transcend. No matter what, don't ever quit! Quitting is not an alternative for a brave soul like yours.

Wherever you are, *LOVE* is. The final death of your preconceived mistaken beliefs and false expectations is the "rising" of your soul. It will allow your eyes to see the truth and to feel the force of real love and true power—the force that created you. For true love is a function, a way of being. We become a creative force in life when we decide to fully, and responsibly, participate in it. We stop being susceptible to living a life of pretense by fearfully following—we become ONE with the energy of Love.

As we become One with this force that created us, we feel its passion and strength in our life. We function and use the power of *LOVE* as our "actions and results speak louder than words." It is here where the journey begins, the everlasting youthful adventure that we have longed for and deeply desired. Where there are no losers; only winners. There is no return. There is only the present and a promising future. As we enter into the state of inner peace, we feel whole and complete. Life then takes anothcr toll, a high-speed motion of endless possibilities of which we never before dreamed, but deep down we always knew it!

The Point of No Return

Once your eyes are open, you will see. You won't be able to go back. You won't be able to deny and deceive yourself anymore. The myth and veils will slowly come down, and then you will see. Your heart will be filled with compassion that brings a deep understanding. You will then rejoice in its presence . . . You are ONE.

Resources

California Government
Social and Mental Health Services
www.ca.gov
Ph: 211-Info Line

San Diego County Health Services
Community Resources-Counseling
www.211sandiego.org
Ph: 211

Victim's Assistance Program
www.sdcda.org
(619) 531-4041

California Partnership to End Domestic Violence
www.caadv.org
(800) 524-4765

Author can be contacted at www.ginaramirez.com